MORE HAUNTED GETTYSBURG

EYE
WITNESS ACCOUNTS
OF THE
SUPERNATURAL

---

by
Jack Bochar
Bob Wasel

Published
by
Donny Bayne

Contents

To Sarah
BW

To Trevor and Molly Burlington
JRB

PREFACE

In the first *Haunted Gettysburg* book, some important thoughts relating to ghosts, haunts, the supernatural, etc., were discussed in the preface. Because those thoughts have not changed and, because the subject matter of the book is identical to the first, it was felt that the original preface should be retained and transferred to this work to inform people of some of the possible reasons certain abnormalities occur. Therefore, we feel the following is worth repeating.

Have you ever had a strange 'feeling' or experienced *Déjà vu* while on the Gettysburg battlefield? Perhaps you thought you saw someone or something that vanished inexplicably before your eyes, or maybe you heard voices and sounds where, plainly no one was visible. Why do so many people report strange occurrences on the battlefield of Gettysburg? It seems the town has far more than its share of supernatural incidents, almost all in some way connected to the battle. Those affected can be men, women, or children, just about anybody who ventures onto the hallowed grounds, ever-soaked with the blood of thousands. Some of these soldiers ended their natural lives suddenly, others lingered painfully until gasping their last breath. Why then, is Gettysburg so abundantly haunted?

With the circumstances surrounding the Battle of Gettysburg, one can see many reasons. Look at some of these conditions. Most of the soldiers were young, no more than mere teenagers. When a man is older, he begins to take on characteristics both physically and mentally to prepare him inevitably for death. As his face takes on wrinkles and his hair grays, he knows he is getting closer to 'the beyond' with his body adjusting through the years. When death does come, he is usually more peaceful and accepting of his fate, but when death comes to a young man, he does not accept it as easily. For a young man, so full of life, death is very unfamiliar, probably the furthest thing from his mind, thinking it can never happen to him. So, for many young men who met a violent death at Gettysburg, the change was too abrupt, never expected. It is thought that their soul is less at rest and not at peace, and therefore, their spirit remains forever where they died, until they can make peace. Another reason spirits are thought to haunt is that when a person dies in unfamiliar surroundings, as did thousands of Union and Confederate soldiers hundreds of miles from home, they roam the fields searching for their homes or friends. One reason they so haunt the battlefield, occurs when a person dies a violent death, such as the scores of men that fell at Gettysburg. It has been said that when a violent death occurs, the spirit of the person goes into a nearby inanimate object, such as a rock or boulder. When one looks at the number of casualties and vast number of rocks on the battlefield, such as the front of Little Round Top and Devil's Den, it is conceivable that each rock could contain the restless spirit of a soul lost to the tragic battle. It is no wonder then, that there is such an abundance of spiritual activity so frequently taking place on old battlefields. This book was written to share a number of people's encounters with the bizarre, unexplainable, or supernatural spirits on the battlefield of Gettysburg.

This project required the assistance of many and we are very thankful to all who have contributed. We wish to acknowledge those who provided generous help, Mary Adelsberger, Sharon Baker, Diane Bochar, Pat Small, and Sarah Richardson. Without their help, in the form of editorial assistance, suggestions on the format of the book, stories, etc., this book could not have been written. Special thanks to Donny and Becky Bayne, for without their assistance and support this book would not have been possible. And to all the kind people who so graciously contributed the stories, we thank you.

INTRODUCTION

Of all the places in the United States, perhaps none can offer as many ghost stories as Gettysburg, Pennsylvania. It seems there is a never-ending supply of people's tales — hearing noises, hearing voices, strange feelings, cold feelings, seeing apparitions, encountering spirits — and the list goes on. The stories have been going on as long as people can remember, and there does not seem to be any slowing down of incidents. Who are these people? Do they have special supernatural abilities? The answer is, the people are *you*. Reports have come in from men, women, young children, seniors, doctors, military personnel, factory workers, psychologists, farmers, people from both high- and low-income jobs. Fact is, it can happen to anyone. For many, they were non-believers — until they came to Gettysburg — now they swear ghosts do exist. It seems a substantial number of Civil War reenactors make contact with spirits, perhaps because their uniform is a very familiar sight to the lingering apparitions.

In this book, it was decided to give the reading audience first-hand stories submitted to the authors. Included are stories from children, reenactors, professionals, etc., to show the wide range of people having some type of strange occurrence or encounter. Rather than rewrite each story, they are, for the most part, presented to you as they were received. Some small editorial changes and additional information were injected to assist in conveying the stories. Most of the stories have taken place recently and it is left entirely up to the reader whether or not that individual believes in ghosts. Because these stories were received from the submitters, the authors cannot claim them as factual. However, by the same token, they cannot deny the stories took place either! It is left to your judgment and beliefs whether or not you choose to believe them. The stories are meant solely for your entertainment and enjoyment.

THE EYES HAVE IT

[Author's commentary]

The Eyes.

We have been asked many times about the eyes on the cover of *Haunted Gettysburg*. The answer to that question goes back a number of years ago when we decided to do a book about the supernatural and Gettysburg. We knew we needed something on the cover to convey a feeling about the contents of the book to the readers. We decided on a pair of eyes with an intense and haunting look. We knew ordinary eyes would never do, so we started building up a file of dozens of eyes from the famous to infamous — good, bad, and obscure people — people who changed history, magicians, religious, powerful, and the unheard of. These people had the most compelling eyes we have ever seen. They varied greatly, but all had one thing in common — eyes you could not ignore — eyes that could change people for the better or for the worse. We then put the eyes in a computer to make a composite. The result is what you see on the cover. We have had people swear they know who the eyes belong to, yet each is a different person. Perhaps that comes from within oneself.

We have received many letters from people telling about a

haunting experience they had. Two of the letters were concerning the eyes on the cover. One person wrote telling us he purchased the book while on vacation in Gettysburg to have something to read while at the motel. He began reading in the evening until about 9:30 PM, when he closed the book. He wanted to get to sleep because he was planning to leave early in the morning. He looked at the cover for a few more moments, or so he thought, but when he again looked up at the clock, he was amazed to see it was 11:30 PM! Somehow, while gazing at the cover, he lost two hours — and he definitely was not sleeping. In another letter, a woman wrote to say she, too, was mysteriously drawn to the cover. She said she had the feeling the eyes were conveying in a strange way, the horrors of the battle. Finally, her husband came into the room and saw her just staring and called to her several times. Eventually she was drawn out of her trance. He told her he did not know where she was, but she certainly wasn't there with him.

It appears many people see different images while looking at the eyes. It is very individual. So do not be surprised if you are certain you see a particular person, while someone else disputes your claim and claims they, in fact, know who it is. We do know that even we find ourselves staring and drawn to the eyes on occasion. Perhaps there is more power to the composite than we can imagine.

GHOSTLY GEOMETRY

[Submitted by: Pauline Hartmann]

After visiting the Triangular Field area so many times before, and having had nothing ever happen to any of our camera equipment, as many of the stories tell, we decided to try our newly purchased video camera to see what might happen there. My brother-in-law, Jerry, having lived in Gettysburg and having contributed many of his own stories of the area, accompanied our family there. He advised me of different camera angles that might contribute to any paranormal activity, but nothing happened. Jokingly, I even dared the spirits to make an appearance — but again — nothing happened. As we all made our way to the back of the field, we saw the "triangle shape" of the ground. As we walked over this boundary, we felt a coldness. Not a chill, but the same coldness you get when opening your freezer! Outside this boundary was a nice warmness from the sun, but inside it was a definite cold! I thought it was my imagination, but my son and daughter also mentioned how "weird" this was. But again, being very skeptical, I felt that there had to be a logical explanation for this phenomenon. I bravely made a statement to Jerry that I felt that these "ghost stories" were made up for the *entertainment* of the tourists."

At the end of our visit to the Triangular Field, we were all in need of something cold to drink, so we decided to go to a local Inn. Having been at the Inn a few times before, we always seemed to pick the same table in the back corner. As I was sitting at the table recapping the day and the coldness in "The Field," I felt the strap of my purse sliding down my arm from the shoulder it was resting on. As I picked it up to place it on the table next to me, I noticed that the strap on the one side was no longer attached to the purse. This somewhat irked me, because it was a fairly new purse and I did not use it very often. Because the Inn was dimly lit, I presumed that the loop at the end of the strap broke and had come off the metal ring on the purse itself. Feeling the strap, I discovered that it was not broken in any way and thought that it must be the metal ring that the strap was attached to. There must have been an opening of some sort in the ring, I thought. I planned to check into this when we got outside

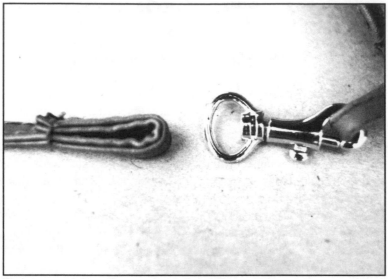

The strap and ring. To reconnect, the strap would have to be unsewn and re-inserted through the ring, then sewn together again.

into the sunlight.

While we walked across the parking lot to our cars, we were planning what we were going to do next. My daughter and I got into our car before anyone else. I decided to investigate this "purse incident" while we waited for Joe, my husband, to get into the car. I checked the metal ring on the purse. There was no slit of any kind in it for anything to slip through! I checked out the strap again — and found it to be perfectly intact! How could this happen? There was absolutely no logical way to explain how this strap could come out of the ring! As Joe was getting into the car, I asked him if he could explain it. He called Jerry over to the car to show him. Neither of them could explain it! Jerry did say though that I shouldn't have doubted the presence of any ghosts anywhere on the battlefield. This possibly angered them!

Is there a logical explanation or is this really the work of a ghost? I say there has to be a reason this happened — but to everyone else, it is

4

the work of an angry spirit from the Triangular Field.

Looking into the Triangular Field.

CAUGHT BETWEEN TWO WORLDS

[Submitted by: Michael Bartholomew]

My name is Michael and this past Spring I graduated from Mount Saint Mary's College in Emmitsburg, Maryland. I had fallen in love with the area after the four years I spent here and decided that I was not quite ready to leave yet. So, I rented an apartment and as exercise, I would often take walks through various areas of the battlefield. Over the four years I spent in the area, one of my roommates and I would often journey to the battlefield and hike, squeezing our way through the caves at Devil's Den; we even had a mock battle using snowballs on Culp's Hill. Nothing out of the ordinary ever happened to me on the excursions until the eighth day of July, 1996. I am documenting this experience while it is still fresh in my memory.

I wanted to feel, even if in a small way, how Longstreet's men felt when marching on Little Round Top. So, I parked my car just off of the Emmitsburg Road and began to walk along Confederate Avenue toward the Round Tops. As I began my walk, I could hear thunder rumbling in the distance; the sky was clouded over, but I decided to chance it. I had wanted to walk this route all day, and I was determined to make it to the Twentieth Maine monument. As I made my way to this position, I remember thinking what good shape Longstreet's men must have been in to reach Gettysburg, unfed and poorly clothed, make a long counter-march to their new position, and perform an uphill attack on the Union lines. By the time I got there I was tired out and I was wearing shorts and a tee-shirt— not a wool uniform— and not toting a gun! Nevertheless, I charged the last 100 feet or so up to the Twentieth Maine monument. I saw some breastworks I had never seen before, so I went to examine them. After poking around for a while, I decided to leave before I got caught in

7

any storms, although it appeared to be clearing in the distance.

I started to head back and, along the way, I picked up a branch that was an excellent size for a walking-stick. This walking-stick also doubled as an excellent "pretend" rifle, so I held it as one and, every once in a while, I'd bring it up to my shoulder as if I was firing, imagining what it must have been like. The thunder was rumbling louder now so I knew I should hurry back. There weren't too many people on that part of the battlefield at this time, because of the weather and the lateness of the hour.

Marker pointing to the area Michael heard the rumbling sounds and artillery blasts.

As I made my way across Plum Run bridge, my curiosity got the best of me. I noticed an interesting outcropping of rocks in the water, so I went into the woods. Just as I began to kneel down to look into the stream, I heard a gentle rumble coming out of the woods to my right. That is what first caught my attention. As I began to look up, the next series of noises made me wheel around very quickly. Four separate and distinct blasts came out of the woods now directly in front of me. I have heard many thunder claps in my life, and I can assure you that this was unlike any I ever heard. The thing that is so eerie is that these blasts came from

8

in the woods, not from the sky. They were so distinct that when each blast went off I could quickly turn my head to the point of that particular explosion. The first thought that came into my head was not "thunder," as would be expected, but "artillery." After the final blast, I waited maybe a second in pure shock and then took off running. I was filled with an

Plum Run Bridge

immense panic! I didn't head toward where I had come off the road, but through the woods to where I could see a road ahead. There was no way I was going toward those sounds. I wanted to get out of that vicinity as fast as possible! As I was "retreating," a feeling hit me that I had never experienced before. It was almost as if electric currents were moving through my body — it is hard to explain. It started in my neck then spread throughout my body giving me goose bumps everywhere. I honestly felt as if something were bearing down on me. Knowing that people say their body feels electrified before getting hit by lightning, I half expected to be hit by lightning. It was unlike anything I ever felt. At certain times, I was scared to the point of almost breaking down into tears.

I hit the road and took off at a sprint. As I rushed past the statue of General Wells, I felt as if he was watching me — I'm not sure if in a positive or negative manner, but I felt eyes on me. I blurted out "Help me!

9

Help me!" as I ran past. If anyone was around, I must have looked foolish; but at that point I didn't really care what anyone, living or dead, thought of me. I was sort of relieved when I hit the clearing near the right of the Confederate line and slowed to a fast walk. I also saw a car parked

Statue of General Wells

by the side of the road, so I felt somewhat safer. By this time it had started to rain. I prayed to God to just let me get back to my car. When I finally reached the car, I got in, locked the doors, and just sat. I felt a sense of relief, but, as soon as I wiped the rain from my glasses and defogged my car windows, I was out of there! I was pretty shaken up but did not tell anyone for fear of ridicule and non-belief.

The next day was bright and sunny, so I got up the nerve to go back. I approached the area where "it" had occurred and parked. I walked up to a marker that I did not remember seeing the night before. It said something to the effect of *5th New York Cavalry* and *Battery E, 4th U.S. Artillery* and sure enough, an arrow pointed off to a path in the woods. Still nervous, and once again alone, I knew what I had to do. At least, this time the sunshine cast a peaceful and friendly glow through the trees. When I reached the top of a hill, not too far from the road, I saw the cavalry marker and then the marker I was looking for. Sure enough, the position of Battery E was looking down on where I had been at Plum Run. When I went back down to the road, I kept an eye on where the marker was and realized the sounds had come from that general area. That Battery had four three-inch guns up there on July 3rd, 1863, and were ready to engage the enemy. As can be expected, I read it with mixed emotions. Part of me hoped that there were four guns and part of me was scared to death that there were. Were the four blasts I heard Battery E opening up on me? Perhaps they thought they saw one of the Confederates, a skirmisher coming to meet General Farnsworth's Cavalry as they charged into the Plum Run Valley on that July day so very long ago. Perhaps the rumble previous to the four blasts was the Union Cavalry riding through the woods, leaping stone walls and charging toward the Confederates. Was that eerie feeling which gripped me, Farnsworth's Cavalry bearing down on what they took to be a vulnerable Confederate? After all, I had wanted to feel what it was like to be one of Longstreet's men marching into battle. Even though July 3rd was not the day I was thinking of, perhaps someone or something didn't think I was getting a vivid enough picture and tried to give me a strikingly clear taste of battle, or at least how frightening it was. Well, you won't ever find me on any part of the battlefield again if I'm alone and in the rain. This happened on July 8th and I am still pretty shaken up. I jump at the slightest unexpected noise. I am shivering and getting goose bumps as I remember and write this and it is hot and humid out. I just wanted to get this extraordinary experience down on paper before the particulars started to fade. Although I have never been so frightened in all my life, I do feel extremely lucky that I was given the chance to peer through this window in time.

THE GUARDIANS OF DEVIL'S DEN

[Submitted by: Wayne Krause]

I just finished reading *Haunted Gettysburg* and was prompted to write about an experience my wife and I had this past June (1996) in Gettysburg.

We had just finished a delightful dinner at one of the long-time local restaurants and my wife suggested we drive through the battlefield

Curve in the road Wayne and his wife first saw the Confederate soldiers.

before it closed for the night. We entered the battlefield by the Peach Orchard around 9:30 PM As we proceeded to Devil's Den, we both noted how quiet, peaceful, and subdued the night was, especially for an area that was known for death and destruction.

With no other vehicles or people in the area, we slowly drove across the field to Devil's Den. As we followed the road that surrounds the boulders, we came to a rise in the road, then saw in the distance coming toward us, a troop of soldiers. I described them as soldiers because they were dressed in Confederate attire carrying muskets, marching in a straight line. The lead man was dressed in a gray uniform with a large hat on his head. He had a ghostly stare, and a pale face with a flesh wound on it. The ironic part is the soldiers never moved their stare from my blinding headlights. As I looked in my rear view mirror, I saw nothing. I turned to my wife and responded by saying, "That's somebody playing a sick joke." Possibly it was my response to denial. I was determined to find an explanation to this frightening experience. I then drove around and back through Devil's Den to see if I could find the pranksters. I could not find them on my second run. I was ever more determined, so I drove around a third time. At the exact point of initial contact, we were confronted by the same troops, coming from nowhere—the same man in front and the same troops marching!

As a practicing psychologist and my wife, a nurse, we cannot explain what we saw that night. The next night I saw the book, *Haunted Gettysburg*. In the book the figures that have been seen at Devil's Den are similar to what we experienced. We now plan to visit Gettysburg again the first weekend in August.

AN UNHOLY NOISE

[Submitted by: Diane Kardos]

I am very surprised that I have not seen or heard a story about the little church in the town of Gettysburg[1]. Let me tell you my experience. Being a stout religious person, my husband and I make Service every Sunday. While we are out of town on vacation, my husband Pat "scouts" for the churches so that we may attend Service. Several years ago, during the fall, Pat found a small church in Gettysburg with a morning Service

Church used as a hospital.

that would accommodate our family. From the moment we stepped into the church I felt "uneasy." I didn't like it for some unknown reason. As

---

[1] Editors note: Due to the nature of this story, we felt it best to leave the church unnamed.

soon as the Service started, so did the noise! Pat's boyhood church had a kitchen in the basement to supply weddings, funerals, and whatever else needed for cooking. Thinking that this was the same setup, I couldn't believe the racket someone was making. Loud bangs and talking could be heard throughout the church while the Service was being offered. I was so upset by the uncalled for action of whomever was making such a racket, that I started to look around to see where the sound was actually coming from. What surprised me was that no one else was bothered by this, including my own family. After Service was over I couldn't get out of the church fast enough. I asked my family, "how could they stand such racket and talking without being disturbed?" To my surprise neither my husband nor my two children had heard anything. I had told them what sounds — loud sounds — I had heard, but once again they stated they heard nothing.

Later that day while touring the fields of battle, Pat started talking to a visitor about the church in the town. To my surprise, and Pat's, we learned that the church was used as a hospital during the Civil War. I had no knowledge of this. Since that day, I have never gone back into that church! I have told Pat that I will wait on the steps, but I will never enter that church again!

DON'T AIM THAT AT ME!

[Submitted by: Kathy Carlton]

Triangular Field.

Each battle site has an aura of its own, and in the Triangular Field at Gettysburg I felt uncomfortable—not frightened—just uneasy.

My sister and I ran into a Civil War reenactor, and I wanted to get a picture of him standing on one of the large, flat rocks that dot the landscape in that area. I had him dead in my sights — the perfect picture. I tried to press the button but it wouldn't budge. Like a brave soldier who stands his ground, the button would not be moved. Our reenactor friend gave it a try, but had the same problem. I had been told about people experiencing difficulties with cameras in that area, but I never thought that

I would be one of the field's "casualties." We tried taking a picture in a different area outside the Triangular Field, and the camera cooperated.

I have never really believed in ghosts or spiritual things, much-less the stories of those who claim to have had run-ins with those who come in and out of unseen dimensions.

Something happened that late Spring afternoon. Perhaps some poor soldier still fighting a battle he cannot escape, decided he didn't want whatever I was holding aimed at him.

Kathy tried to photograph the reenactor on this rock.

Whatever or whomever dwells in that space of never-ending time, if indeed anything at all exists there, may have been the reason for the uneasiness I felt in the Triangular Field, where all too many brave men gave up their last full measure of devotion, so many years ago.

After returning home, the camera was placed on a table by a lamp. Strangely, the light in the lamp flickered. By mere chance, I removed the camera from the table and the light stopped flickering. I didn't think there was any connection between the lamp and the camera until I again placed it by the lamp. Sure enough, the light flickered! Some people say spirits can go into objects. In this case, I hope it is NOT true and hope that I did not bring anything home with me from the Triangular Field!

-6-

I SHOULD HAVE LISTENED

[Submitted by: Ashley Ott]

Legend has it Pauline Noel "burned" her name in this rock.

I am ten years old and I went to the battlefield with my grandpa, who wanted to show me where P. Noel took her fire-burning finger and carved her name in a rock. In the book, *Haunted Gettysburg*, it tells you that if you take your finger and trace the letters in P. Noel's name on the rock, then you will have bad luck. But, I thought that was unreal so I did it. I took my finger and traced P. Noel's name. Now all these strange things started happening to me. That very night I was walking on the sidewalk and I fell off the curb and I got a big scrape on my knee. The next day I was walking down some cement stairs and I fell. I got a big scrape on my shin, a scratch on my other knee and a scratch on the knee

19

I fell on first. On my left arm I got a brush burn. I felt I was cursed for tracing the letters of P. NOEL, so I returned and put a penny on Penny Rock for luck.

Arrow shows location of the "P. Noel" rock, adjacent to Smith's 4th New York Battery.

THE LOST BOYS

[Submitted by: Chuck W. Caldwell]

The following event happened to me November 12, 1984. It was 8:15 AM on a clear and crisp Fall day. Walking in a southeasterly direction around Culp's Hill, the leaves had fallen from the trees and only dry leaves bordered that section of East Confederate Avenue.

In front of me were three hatless boys, two with tan coats, the center boy with a dark blue coat. From behind they appeared to be of high

Photo taken by Chuck Caldwell November 12, 1984 at 9:15 a.m.

school age and my "warning system" turned on. I thought, "these people are skipping school". They were quiet — no talking, no smoking — just walking, and I was very soon going to overtake them.

I mentally prepared myself for anything that might happen, using my belt and buckle if necessary, since they soon would be behind me and I didn't intend to be defenseless. About ten yards past the Daniel's Brigade plaque, with my eyes fixed on the three people, without movement or sound, they suddenly disappeared.

I looked all around the area and realized it would have been impossible for them to have jumped from the road to behind the trees, especially not without a sound since the brown dried leaves would allow me to hear a squirrel many yards away in the woods.

Not believing my eyes, I continued my walk and decided to return. I retraced my steps, armed with a camera, exactly one hour later. The camera showed that the road was clearly visible, dropping off slightly to the right and then leading to the left to a rise where the road was completely visible. There was no place for anyone to jump into any woods!

Photo taken by author at the same spot of previous photo, November 12, 1996.

-8-

SOUNDS OF SILENCE

[Submitted by: Bob Wasel]

     The winter of 1995/96 was a time of change for Tom Winter, Sr. and Tom Winter, Jr., owners of Time Line Photo, an old time photo studio located in the Old Gettysburg Village. The Winters were moving next door into a new and larger studio. With Spring quickly approaching, there were just a few finishing touches to be made, one of which was to wire some speakers for Civil War music to play both inside and outside of the studio to add to the flavor of their business. They had asked me to do the wiring, since I had experience as an electrician. The job was quickly done, and it was time to test the system. I brought over one of my favorite audio tapes that I had listened to many times before. We placed the tape

Voices can be heard from these speakers outside the shop.

into the tape player, but instead of music, out came the voice of Tom Sr. Initially, we were both quite taken aback. Tom said, "What am *I* doing in there?" I told him I thought we made a mistake and accidentally taped his voice over the music. I rewound the tape to the beginning and tried it again. This time the music played and there was no voice.

I initially thought we recorded Tom's voice by accident, but on close inspection realized the tape was "play-only" and the tape player had no microphone for recording — there was no way what happened should have! From time to time Tom Jr. has reported hearing voices intermingled with the music. If you come by the studio and the music is playing, listen very closely — there may be a voice that talks to you.

JACKSON'S STRANGE ENCOUNTER

[Submitted by: Donna L. Curran]

My family and I visit Gettysburg three or four times per year. This year, 1996, over the July 4th holiday, we brought our dog with us, a one-and-a-half year old Golden Retriever named Jackson. We were staying, as usual, at an motel on Steinwehr Avenue. Jackson and I would get up every morning at 5:30 AM and walk across the High Water Mark. The first few days, we went around through the Visitor's Center/Cyclorama walkway, and all was fine — until I changed my course.

"Jackson", the Golden Retriever that became enraged at the *111th NY* monument.

On about the fourth day of our visit, I began walking Jackson up the road past the Bryan Farm. Next to the barn is a monument to the 111th New York Infantry depicting a soldier on top of a granite base. As we got near it, Jackson went crazy!!! I'm sure you know that Goldens are very placid, laid-back dogs, and Jackson is no different. He doesn't bark, growl, or show any other forms of aggression, ever. He is very loving and trusting, but this monument did something to him. He

111th New York Monument "Jackson" barked at.

hunkered down, growling, his hackles standing straight-up on end. Through all his training, we have been told to get to the root of any aggressive behavior, should there be a need. Therefore, I tried to get him to walk over to the monument, sniff it, and see that there was nothing to be scared of, or upset by. He would have none of it. He tugged on his leash, whined, barked, and just completely broke down.

At this point, we continued on our walk, and he was fine. I intentionally walked him past as many monuments with soldiers atop them as possible. We went over to the Meade monument — nothing. We went to other monuments around the "Angle" and the Pennsylvania monument — nothing. However, on the way back, past the Bryan Farm again, he had the same reaction. He went crazy. There were no other people or animals there, just the monument.

For the remainder of our trip, I took him all over the battlefield. I took him on a walk of the field of Pickett's Charge. I took him to Little Round Top — nothing — he was absolutely fine. I continued to walk him past the Bryan Farm, and each time he had the very same reaction, with the barking, crying, crawling, and tugging. I am convinced that there was something there, something that scared him very much. Jackson is a wonderful dog, very true to his breed and is extremely well-trained. He just had never acted the way he did at the Bryan Farm, and he hasn't acted that way since.

I myself had no uncomfortable feelings at all during any of our walks, even though some mornings it was rainy, foggy, or just downright spooky. I have heard it said that some dogs and other animals are very sensitive to strange feelings, etc., and I believe that Jackson experienced it first-hand.

–10–

PICKETT'S ETERNAL CHARGE

[Name withheld by request]

Jim and five of his friends finally got around to doing something every Civil War buff dreams about — to walk the field where Pickett made his famous charge. Not quite a mile across, it is one of the most emotional places of any battlefield of any war. Whether you are from the

Area of Pickett's Charge.

North or the South, it is impossible to walk that field without a deep sense of pride that you are an American. There was unimaginable courage on both sides of the field on that hot day of July 3, 1863. The Southern

27

soldier may have failed to take the Union position that day, but they went down in history as some of the finest and bravest warriors any country ever produced.

Area of Pickett's Charge.

It was a perfect fall day when Jim and his friends stepped off from the Virginia monument to try to get a feel for what it was like for those soldiers so long ago. They had not gone far when they started hearing noises that were not being made by them. The sounds they heard were coming from behind, but kept getting closer all the time. They recognized it as the sounds soldiers make when on the march. The coordinated footsteps of determined men, the creak of leather, tin cups rattling, the distinctive sound a saber makes when hanging on a man's side. Soon the sounds were all around them and even occupied the same space as their physical bodies, then moved past and beyond. Those six men now tell their friends they not only walked Pickett's Charge but were allowed by the spirits to *participate* in the charge for a few moments.

Another similar story we heard recently is about Steve, from Ohio, who visits Gettysburg whenever he gets a chance — sometimes just a quick trip. On a three-day weekend, Steve got up early one beautiful Fall day with the express purpose of being alone on the battlefield and walking Pickett's Charge. It was the beginning of a perfect day as Steve started his walk. There were small patches of fog and the field was still wet with dew. It was quiet and Steve was alone with his thoughts — just what he wanted. Not long after he started his walk he, too, heard noises. It was the sound of men marching on either side of him. He said it was like soldiers were forming up around him and he was part of their brigade. For some strange reason, Steve did not turn around, but went with the feeling, and headed for the High Water Mark. He said as he got closer the spirits or beings seemed to drop away and when he reached the "angle" he was alone again.

There are those who say you cannot march Pickett's Charge alone. The spirits of those brave men will fall in with you, still obeying their orders given so long ago — destined to make that charge again and again for all time, but unable to go any further than those places where their earthly bodies fell on that bloody day of July 3, 1863.

-11-

OUT OF THE DARKNESS

[Submitted by: Lori Thompson]

I was traveling east on Wheatfield Road on my way to the house of my boss, Bob Servant. I called Bob from the car phone to tell him I was on my way, when up ahead I saw movement of shadows off to the right in the field. I slowed the van down because I thought it was a deer and since I was driving Bob's van, I did not want to wreck it. As I got closer, I saw two figures emerging from the direction of the brush about fifty feet from the road. All of a sudden it started getting very bright — more than the brightness of the high-beams from the van. There was a bright glow. I couldn't talk and Bob kept saying, "Are you okay?" Finally, I was able to tell him to hold on and not to hang up. He knew by the sound of my voice that something very strange was going on.

At this point, two soldiers came walking out of the field toward the road. They looked like they were walking at attention, their chins slightly elevated. They seemed not to notice that I was there, but I had the feeling that they wanted me to notice them. There was a Confederate and a Union soldier. The Confederate soldier was on the left and the Union soldier was on the right. The Union soldier had a mark on his left cheek with black around the outer part of the mark. You could see where blood had run down his face and onto his collar. The Confederate soldier was disheveled and unshaven and had on a light gray shell jacket and sky-blue trousers, black brogans on his feet, and his trousers were tucked into his socks. On his dark brown hat, from what I could make out, it appeared to be either the number "4" or the number "9". He was carrying a haversack. The Union soldier had a sack-coat and an infantry belt and buckle, with a musket over his right shoulder, the sling appeared to be made of heavy twine.

31

Spot where Lori saw two soldiers walking toward her.

I was not afraid of them, but had this feeling of despair and grief — as if their feelings were being passed onto me. The two soldiers walked to where the grass meets the road and stopped as if they could not go beyond that point. After I passed them, it became very dark. The brightness was gone. I traveled on to Bob's house and was as white as a sheet when I arrived. Bob and I drove back to the spot, but there was nothing there — just the stillness and darkness of the night.

-12-

TIME TWINS

[Submitted by: William Benner]

While this is not exactly a "ghost" story, it is bizarre. A few years ago, my wife and I made one of our occasional trips to Gettysburg. During our visit, we strolled up to the Evergreen Cemetery to see the grave of the local, well-known Jenny Wade. After finding her grave, for some strange reason, we continued walking around the area, randomly reading tombstones. I do remember feeling a presence or something but did not think too much about it at the time. All of a sudden, I got the shock of my life —

William Benner's grave (arrow) in proximity to the Jenny Wade grave.

there was a tombstone with MY name on it — William Benner! Then came another shock. The date of birth on the stone was Dec. 20, 1843 — mine is Dec. 20, 1943! It gave me a cold chill like I was looking into my own grave. Yet, it does not quite end there. His wife's name was Nancy — the same as my wife's! I felt like I was in the Charles Dickens classic, *A Christmas Carol*, when Scrooge comes across his own grave.

Grave of William Benner

13

ADRIFT IN TIME

[Submitted by: Carl Bosler]

On July 3, 1995, I was at a reenactment all day on Pumping Station Road. After the day's event, I went home and got cleaned up. I put my full Confederate uniform back on about 9:30 PM and went down to Devil's Den. I climbed up on top of a boulder, propped myself up against a tree, and fell asleep. Something startled me and I woke up — it was about 3 AM. I realized I was sweating profusely. I looked around and saw the top of the hill was now foggy. At this point I noticed that my Alabama Flatlander hat was gone. I searched for my hat but could not find it. There was no breeze blowing so I know it did not blow away.

Carl wearing his "Alabama Flatlander" hat prior to his encounter.

I decided to leave the Den, so I walked to my truck, which was parked nearby. I thought I would return in the morning and look for my hat. When I opened the door of the truck, the cab light came on, and I climbed in, just glancing in the mirror. When I did, I noticed my face was covered with gunpowder residue and there were white streaks down my face from the sweat running down. Then I noticed that my hands were

Tree where Carl slept.

also covered with gunpowder residue. Being covered with sweat and grime and feeling exhausted, I wondered if I fell asleep and into another dimension, only to struggle with those brave Confederates in that desperate battle to take Devil's Den.

I went home and got cleaned up again. I laid down for a while and got up early before the park opened to return and look for my hat. I never found it. I have often wondered about that hat and, after my strange experience, felt anything was possible. Did some Confederate soldier see me lying there and, thinking me dead, take the hat I would never need again? Impossible? Who can say for sure?

Devil's Den.

14

CHRISTMAS FEAR

[Submitted by: Tracy K. Hartman]

It was Christmas Eve and I was closing the bar at The Gingerbread Man restaurant on Steinwehr Ave. I had a late crowd that night which enabled the other closing staff to get a head start on the closing duties. I soon found myself fifteen minutes into the paperwork and alone. Everyone I was working with that night finished much earlier than I and could not stay due to previous holiday obligations. Although I had never been left alone at the Gingerbread Man this late at night before, and had heard many ghost stories about the place, I figured "It's Christmas, a holy day, nothing is going to happen." So I decided to be big

about the whole thing and proceed with my work. I went upstairs to the office and began my paperwork. While there, I kept thinking I was seeing things move out of the corner of my eye. Knowing it was just my mind playing tricks on me, I still found myself saying

The *Gingerbread Man Restaurant.*

37

aloud, "Please just leave me alone, I'm almost done and then I'll be gone!" After about an hour, I was finally finished and very ready to go home. I only had two things left to do — check the front and side doors, and set the computer up for the next day. When I got downstairs, I went straight to the front door, checked — it was locked. Then I went to the side door, which is located in the bar, checked — it, too, was locked. But, when I turned around, to my horror, I found that there was a glass floating in mid-air about five inches away from the glass rack! It stayed there, with me frozen in fright for about three seconds, until it finally dropped, shattering. It didn't just fall to the floor — it was as if the glass were slammed down hard by some unseen hand. I instantly started to scream but made myself stop for fear of upsetting whatever or whomever was there with me. I then remembered I still had to set the computer, which required going behind the bar where the glass had just crashed to the floor. I took a deep breath and began to slowly walk over. Upon rounding the bar to go behind it, I could feel all the hairs on the back of my neck stand on end and instant goose bumps were over my entire body. I moved toward the computer, hearing the glass crunch under my shoes. I tried several times to set the computer but was too shaken up. I just could not do it. I decided that since we'd be closed the following day, I would come in then and clean up the broken glass, as well as run some reports on the computer. However, when I arrived the next day, I found all the glass had mysteriously been moved to the other side of the computer. Was a spirit angered at the prospect of being alone again at Christmas?

-15-

UNFORGETTABLE GOODBYE

[Submitted by: Debbie Shutt]

The glass flew from this rack.

Mary Beth had been working at the Gingerbread Man longer than any other wait-staff there. She was finally going back to college, something she was planning to do for five long years. Then it came — the last day of work — and we were standing at the bar, talking about how strange it would be without her there. Suddenly, a glass from the end of the bar where Mary Beth was standing, unexplainably flew off the brass glass-rack above us, smashing onto the floor! It was almost like the "Ghost of the Gingerbread Man" wanted to say goodbye in its own mysterious way.

Loaves of bread fly from this rack.

These are not isolated incidents, as numerous unexplained stories have been told concerning the Gingerbread Man. Employees many times have seen figures of people out of the corners of their eyes—this is not an uncommon occurrence. Some employees, while working in the kitchen where the bread is stored, have seen a loaf of bread fly out of the bread holder.

16

VOICES FROM THE PAST

[Submitted by: Mary Adelsberger]

It was a cold, cloudy February afternoon. My daughters, Ann, 27, and Jen, 22, and I had plans for a weekend in Gettysburg. The forecast called for a heavy snowfall, but that did not deter us. It would take a lot more than a mere blanket of snow to keep us away from the town we had fallen in love with over the past few months.

We had reservations at the quaint and lovely Bed and Breakfast, Doubleday Inn, located right on the battlefield. We arrived at the Inn at approximately 3:00 PM; by the time we unpacked, settled in, and familiarized ourselves with our surroundings, it was about 5:30 PM. After a leisurely drive through the battlefield and many purchases at the various shops in town, we decided to stop for dinner. We dined at an historic restaurant, where we lingered for about an hour and a half. At 8:00 PM we stopped at a local pub, where we met some friends for a couple of drinks. We left there about 10:00 PM, at which time it was snowing quite heavily — at least five inches had already accumulated. We marveled at the sight! The town truly looked like a "ghost town," as we were the only ones on the road. We decided to take advantage of the situation, and drove up and down all roads that were accessible. About 11:00 PM, we headed back to the Inn. During our drive back, we remarked on how exceptionally beautiful the battlefield appeared, covered by the sparkling snow.

After we arrived back at the Inn, Ann and Jen came up with a brilliant idea — "Let's take a walk," they said. Feeling tired, and not exactly sharing in their enthusiasm, I told them to go ahead — that I preferred to stay at the Inn and kick back with a good book in front of the fireplace. They had originally planned to just walk across the road, where there are several monuments. They were curious about them. Instead, once they got outside, they decided to go left on Doubleday Avenue, and walked until they came to Wadsworth Avenue, where they turned right. Shortly after they were on Wadsworth, Jen saw something in the snow — it was a marker at the edge of the woods. She walked over to it, brushed off the snow, and let out a quiet sigh. It said "95th New York Infantry ... July 1, 1863."

Almost immediately, they heard what appeared to be the sounds of men's voices — singing, as if they were sitting around a campfire. They then heard what sounded like muffled voices — "idle talk," as they described it — coming from deep in the woods. They looked at each other, to make sure they were both hearing the same thing. They stood motionless for a few moments, not really knowing what to do. At first, they thought maybe it was a couple of pranksters, but dismissed that idea, thinking, "who else but we would be crazy enough to go out on a snowy night like this?" Jen suggested they walk into the woods to see what — or whom — may be there. Ann was not exactly thrilled with that notion but, seeing Jen heading into the woods, she quickly followed. As they walked, they heard not only voices, but also a sound which they described as the sound a belt would make if you held it upside down and shook it. As they got even further into the woods, they heard a loud "crack" coming from their right. They looked over in the direction from which the sound came, where they 'thought' they saw a large boulder, illuminated by a bluish hue. But they saw nothing. Suddenly, they heard one voice yell out above the rest: "GET UP! GET UP! GO! GO!" This was followed by the command, "CHARGE!" At this point, Jen fell to her knees in fear (although to this day she swears she tripped!). As they were frantically looking for their way back to the road, they heard the sounds of men screaming and moaning. They looked at each other and bolted from the woods as fast as their legs would take them!

At approximately 12:30 AM, they arrived back at the Inn — Ann in tears and Jen talking a mile a minute! Fearing the worst, I asked what had happened. We went to our room and they relayed to me what had happened. They pleaded with me to accompany them back to the woods, in order to prove to themselves that they weren't crazy. I wasn't exactly enthusiastic about the idea, but I knew if I didn't go back with them, none of us would get any sleep that night! I agreed to go with them, but with a couple of stipulations: we would *drive*, not walk; I would *not* get out of the car; and one of them had to promise to stay in the car with me at all times! I also suggested to Jen that it might be wise to take the video camera, just in case it picked up any sounds. Upon agreeing to my stipulations, we left for the woods.

We turned onto Wadsworth Avenue, stopping near the 95th New York Infantry marker. Jen opened the car door, stepped out, and before she even had a chance to close the door, I heard it — the most horrible, blood-curdling screams and moans that anyone could possibly imagine! A most overwhelming sense of sadness enveloped me, and I immediately

Area Mary and her daughters heard the shouts, screams, and moans.

broke down in uncontrollable tears. I curled up in the back of the car, and screamed, "Get me out of here, make it stop!" Upon hearing my screams, Jen hurried back to the car and we sped away, skidding uncontrollably on the snow-covered road. I don't recall where we drove after that, I only remember that we drove around and around for at least two hours — Ann and I crying all the while. We tried to make sense of it all, but we couldn't. The whole experience was totally unexplainable.

When we arrived back at the Inn, we went to our room and sat in silence. We just looked at each other with blank stares. After a while, we were finally able to talk about it, and conceded that obviously we truly must have had an encounter with "voices from the past."

We felt so sad, so helpless, so powerless — there had to be something we could do to help these poor souls find their way "home." Jen suggested that maybe it would help if we prayed for them. So, we all said our own silent prayer, hoping that they would be released from the pain and suffering they had endured for so long.

The 23rd North Carolina, along with the 5th, 20th, and 12th North Carolina, were ordered, but not led by, Brigadier General Alfred Iverson to take a position at the stone wall to the left and front. At this spot (marked A on map) 600 North Carolina troops were shot down, in a line as straight as their formation, by unseen Union troops behind the wall. A witness said the blood ran like a small creek down the hill to the right of the small monument. They were buried at this spot in mass graves, later known as Iverson's Pits. The grass and crops always grew greener here.

The day after this experience, we scoured the book shops, looking for any information we could about the 95th New York Infantry, still hoping to make sense of it all. We located a book (the title of which escapes me at this time) which *did* confirm part of what Ann and Jen heard. From what I recall, the 95th New York and the 23rd North Carolina were at that location, and both sides suffered heavy losses. In

44

the book, it stated that indeed, there were commands of "GET OUT, GET OUT," and "CHARGE," which was affirmation enough for us to know that what we heard was not just imagined.

We have stopped at the 95th New York Infantry marker a multitude of times since that cold, snowy February night. However, not once since then have we heard any sounds emerging from the woods. Maybe our prayers did, indeed, release those poor, sad souls from the hell they were trapped in for so long and led them into the heavenly light. We can only hope.

Servant's *Olde Time Photos*.

17

STAINS UPON THE FLOOR

[Submitted by: Gina and Kevin Servant]

Major-General John Reynolds, who was commander of the 1st Corps on July 1, 1863, came into Gettysburg with the much-needed reinforcements General Buford desperately requested. As Reynolds arrived, he conferred with Buford on the situation and congratulated him on the superb job in holding back such a large Confederate force. Also, Reynolds approved of the selection of the ground Buford chose to hold the opposing forces back. After initiating a number of dispatches and messages to his generals and officers, Reynolds directed newly arrived troops — the famed *Iron Brigade* — to cut off advances through the woods. These "Black Hatted" men desperately fought off Archer's men, as General Reynolds, on horseback, watched. During the clash, a bullet struck General Reynolds behind the ear. Some witnesses claim he died instantly

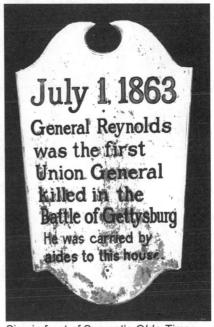

Sign in front of Servant's *Olde Time Photos* building.

as he fell from his horse. The nearby soldiers took the lifeless body of their General back toward town, where they placed him inside a stone home belonging to a local resident. Blood, still coming out of the wound,

Arrow pointing to spot Reynold's blood was reported to have been seen.

began to leak onto the floorboards, leaving a stain where the body lay.

Over the years, a number of people have lived in that home and from time-to-time, businesses were established within its walls. For some of the occupants, strange occurrences have taken place, almost never explained. The current proprietors, Servant's *Olde Time Photos,* have a few incidents of their own. In one instance, during the evening, they found that a shelf located upstairs, with a porcelain horse upon it, mysteriously came off the wall and fell to the floor. This, in itself, does not sound out of the ordinary, but consider the fact that in order for the shelf to be removed, it would be required to lift it over two nails. No way could it have fallen or slid off on its own accord. Not only that, but the shelf was unbroken and the fragile porcelain horse came tumbling down—unbroken and standing upright!

In another instance, Kevin Servant photographed a person in Civil War attire and when the photo was developed, the sword and sword belt appeared on the opposite side of the body from which it was photographed on, as one would see on the old glass-plate photographs.

Recently, a long-time resident came by the *Olde Time Photos* building directing Kevin Servant, along with newspaper reporters, to the very spot where General Reynold's body lay, staining the floor with his blood. As a young boy, he was shown the actual spot and stains by the people who lived in the house at that time. Although the spot can be identified, the bloodstain can no longer be seen because the floor is now concrete.

The unbroken horse.

Where Reynolds fell.

Reynold's grave, Lancaster cemetery - photo courtesy of Douglas Barr.

50

-18-

HISTORIC REFLECTIONS

[Submitted by: Amber Gordon]

My name is Amber Gordon and I am twelve years old. I am a reenactor with the 56th Pennsylvania, Company B.

My interest in the Civil War started a few years ago. I'm especially interested in the generals, soldiers, and battles.

I read *Haunted Gettysburg* and did not put it down until I finished reading it. My favorite story was "Music in a Boy's Eye."

Of all the historic places I have been to, there is something that draws me to Cashtown. Like places on the Gettysburg Battlefield that are special, Cashtown is special to me. Every time we come to Gettysburg, we pass through Cashtown or sometimes stop to take pictures.

When we first went there in July of 1994, I took a picture of the Cashtown Inn, and one of the sign nearby. When the pictures were developed, I realized that there were ghosts in them.

On July 2, 1995, we went through Cashtown again. I took another picture of the sign and I saw a ghost in that one too. Maybe because I took these in July, at or near the time of the battle at Gettysburg, that has something to do with it. When I took the pictures, I did not see anything unusual. I don't know why these ghosts appear in my pictures, unless they want to be seen.

I have shown my pictures to many people—other reenactors, historians, teachers, and anyone who was interested and asked to see them. Everyone has seen the ghosts. Some saw them quicker than others.

Getting ghosts in pictures and seeing ghosts can happen to anyone. I'm proof that kids can get ghost pictures too.

[Editor's note: In looking over Amber's photographs, it seems people see different things. Many see reflections, glares, or ordinary scenes. Who can say that what they see and what Amber sees are the same? Perhaps

51

some people, for some unexplained reason, can actually see things in a photograph that others can't. As we look at the photo, we see a glare and reflection; however, listen to Amber's description: "To the right of the door and below the bulletin board is a bench. Sitting on the bench is a little boy wearing a light shirt and pants with suspenders. He has a wide brimmed hat on his head. He is sitting with his hands together in front of him and his legs are apart. He is looking at two men walking up to the door. The one man is to the left of the door and one in front of it. The man to the left has a side brimmed hat. You can see his collar too." So, you see, Amber's detailed description may be far from what we are able to observe. One explanation is, perhaps some people, for whatever reason , are given the privilege of seeing what others cannot.]

Amber's photograph of *Cashtown Inn* taken July 1994.

52

19

INTO THE OUTER-LIMITS

[Submitted by: Cathe Curtis]

While some people either have or have not experienced any sense of emotion at Devil's Den, the Wheatfield, or any of the other many areas of traumatic battle, I, myself, have always been reduced to a most profound combination of humility, love, awe, and sorrow when treading over such hallowed ground. But for reasons unknown to me, I have been allowed, somehow, to "take a peek" into the horrors of battle from long, long ago — the Battle of Gettysburg.

Upon reaching the summit of rocks at Devil's Den, around 8 PM on a warm, humid evening in early August, 1996, I was immediately drawn to sit upon a most-inviting rock — why that particular rock, I do not know. Maybe because I was unbelievably winded after scaling the rocky crags or, maybe because it was meant to be.

I must admit, at first, I felt somewhat disappointed because there was an unusually large crowd of people, mostly families, with children all about and everywhere, having a grand old time, playing King of the Mountain, jumping, climbing, and parents worrying, warning their children to be careful on the rocks. Then, all of a sudden, the people, the environment all around me, all of the present-day reality, was beginning to totally "phase-out," as if it were being sucked into some giant vacuum! Now I *knew* that reality was most certainly still "there" somewhere, but I no longer "saw" the people or "heard" them. For I was NOW hearing and seeing piercingly loud exchanges of artillery and cannon in the very near distance. I was inhaling an overpowering stench of sulphur, burnt human flesh, and a grand-scale of what smelled like dirty human sweat. I was hearing pathetic muffled moans, pained voices crying out, bloodcurdling screams, and hushed sobs, again and again, one after another, not stopping. I detected the smell and sounds of a light drizzling rain, all the while hearing tin and steel scraping along the rocks all around me and beneath me. In a flash, there they were, those intrepid young men in uniform, blue and gray, most of them tattered and blood-drenched. I don't know why I noticed that most of the men were missing buttons on their jackets and that very few of them were even wearing a cap. There I

Cathe first saw her vision from this rock.

sat, fighting all around me, oblivious at this point of my "real world" which was undoubtedly "somewhere out there". All I did know for sure was that I was in some other world, but not mine. "How long is this going to last?", I fearfully wondered to myself. "And how long have I BEEN here?" "Can these men see me?" All of these questions racing through my mind, witnessing one horror after another. Then I spotted a young man in blue crouching behind a large boulder down below — he seemed to be attempting to hide — to keep out of sight. Perhaps his fear had overcome his bravery. But then a bullet brought him down to his knees, and he fell face-down into a pool of mud. My very last thought was how astonished I was to see so many men in hand-to-hand combat! I had always felt that most of the men had met death through gunshot wounds or from the cannons. But to see them bludgeoning their enemies to death, choking one another, and stabbing their victims with what appeared to be small knives — I couldn't believe what I was seeing before me.

Well, what had seemed to be a long time was most likely only a few minutes, but my "window" into the battle phased-out and diminished as quickly as my own "real world" had done. Reality returned — gleeful shouts of the children at play on the rocks, parents chiding them to be careful not to fall. I slowly turned to my right and saw my fiancé progressing down the path toward me. I immediately debated if I should share this most wonderful experience with him? After all, he was quite used to my "unusual" experiences that I have been having most of my life. But then I decided to hold off, at least for the time being, anyway. I quickly turned my face to the left and wiped away my tears, slowly tricking down my cheeks, after

Tree near the end of small footbridge where Cathe saw the second part of her vision.

seeing the sights of war. We then decided to go into the woods, walking first, over the footbridge. I immediately found myself being pulled to a very large, thick, old tree, located near the end of the footbridge. No sooner had I leaned against the tree when I envisioned a very young, brown-haired Confederate soldier whose left arm was blown right off from his shoulder! I could see each and every detail of the proud flesh then exposed — what a horrible, gaping wound — the gushes of blood seeming to pump out of the hole in his left shoulder, all the while, seeing the raw terror on his young face, grimacing with outlandish pain, and screaming with every breath. He was covered with some kind of dark soot, all over his skin and clothing, and he had dark, little stone-like pieces of what looked like bits of coal, embedded into his face and stuck to his ragged uniform. The next thing I knew, the scene was gone, once again departing as quickly as it had appeared. And then I heard my fiancé calling out to me that he was ready to leave.

Although I have been able to observe, hear, and experience various supernatural phenomena ever since my childhood, never before had reality "phased out" and returned the way it did on this particular day in Gettysburg. Never before had I been swept out of "my world" into another witnessing events as if I had actually BEEN there, events that I shall never, never forget. I am hopeful that these unusual episodes will continue. Needless to say, I am anxious to return many times to Gettysburg and walk upon those hallowed grounds again and again. I'll be looking for that "window" into the past, to 1863. I know that it is there — and I know that I will find it again.

20

SCHOOL FOR THOUGHT

[Submitted by: Rich and Trish Eisenhower]

My wife and I enjoy Gettysburg a great deal, and make a number of trips per year to visit the small town and experience the history of the great battle that was fought there.

During our visit on August 24, 1996, we both decided to take one of the featured Candlelight Ghost tours we had seen advertised.

"Old Dorm".

The tour took in many interesting and historical stops, including a few on the campus of Gettysburg College. Our guide, dressed in period costume of ankle-length, hooped skirt, was very well versed in the origins and ghostly histories of the numerous dwellings we stopped at along the

57

route. One of the sites incorporated in the tour was "Old Dorm" on the Gettysburg College campus.

Our group, comprised of about 23, was sitting on the steps of "Old Dorm" passing around some bullets and musket balls that had been provided by our guide for our inspection. We listened to the story of how "Old Dorm," like many other buildings in the town, had been used as a hospital during and after the hellish and bloody three-day campaign.

Arrows indicating the sites of the first, second, and third sightings.

After finishing her story, our guide led off down the walkway from the steps of "Old Dorm" toward the college theater that stood a short distance away. I had only walked a few feet down the pathway when, for some unknown reason, my attention was drawn to the right. About 30 feet away stood two men at the most rigid, military attention, appearing as if they were about to be inspected. Lights from a nearby college building, which stood behind them, clearly produced, the silhouettes of both men in the deepest, most lustrous ebony I have ever seen.

A taller man stood to the left while a second, a little shorter, stood to the right, as I observed them. Both wore a large, circular brimmed hat that had been favored by infantrymen as protection from sun and rain.

Both men stood as if statues not the slightest movement. In fact, that had been my first impression. Never having been to the campus before, I thought it quite possible that what I was looking at were statues that had been erected by the college.

I had some fast speed film in my camera, and intrigued by the situation, I put the men in the view finder and snapped a picture.

My wife approached me at this time, very excited, and asked if I had seen two men. I confirmed that I did, but didn't realize that she had been referencing a point a few yards from where I had seen them.

We were both excited. But before proceeding to catch up to the group, which had already arrived at the theater, I decided to take a quick walk toward where I had seen the two men to establish whether or not it had been a statue or monument of which I had taken a picture. There was no statue and the men had disappeared!

I thought, possibly, that it may have been part of a college prank, as many students were returning to the college that weekend from summer vacation, but I could not imagine anyone having the ability to stand so still.

After returning to the group, as we were listening to the haunting stories of the college theater, my wife tugged firmly on my sleeve, exclaiming in an excited whisper, "Look! Those men are behind us now!"

Surely they were! A few yards from us in the same manner as we had seen them before, the two ebony shadows stood, at inflexible attention, seemingly watching us. We were about to call their attention to the rest of the group and our guide, but when we looked back to where they stood — they had vanished! We had only looked away from them for a few seconds.

The tour made its way to the town square as the final stop, where we told our guide about our sighting. She was very excited and related a similar experience that she had heard occurred in the same area before.

A second tour group of about 20 people, came into the town square a few minutes later. Our guide called out to the leader of the second group that she believed we had a sighting. The tour guide of the second group, a male also dressed in period costume, called back, "Did they see the men in the large hats?"

My wife and I were really excited. Only four people in the second group had witnessed the silent soldiers, also standing at attention, as they made their way to the theater from "Old Dorm."

I since have had the film developed that I took that evening. I have a picture of some trees profiled against the light that is radiating from one of the campus buildings of Gettysburg College, but there is nothing else in the picture. I've had an enlargement made as a reminder of a wonderful and enlightening experience. I know when I took the picture, two soldiers who fought gallantly over one-hundred-thirty-three years ago, stood silently at attention, looking on from another dimension.

[Author's Note: The same two soldiers have also been reported to us through other people.]

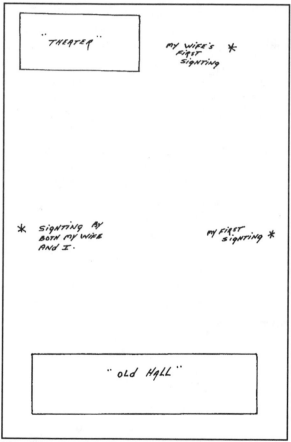

Map drawn by Rich Eisenhower showing areas of their sightings.

21

HOT TIME IN THE OLD TOWN

[Submitted by: Beth Brett]

[Author's Note: For those not familiar with the Dobbin House, we thought a short background on it would be appropriate. It is Gettysburg's oldest building, built in 1776. Alexander Dobbin, a short and stout man, born in Ireland in 1742, met and married Isabella Gamble. Together, the couple left Ireland and sailed to America. They made their way to the area and Alexander became a minister in a church about a mile from Gettysburg. A very early pioneer in the area, Reverend Alexander Dobbin, instrumental in the founding of Gettysburg, purchased 300 acres situated in the future town of Gettysburg. There, in 1774 Dobbin began

The Dobbin House.

61

construction of his house.

Dobbin built a large home to accommodate his family and to double as a school. Not only was the house large, but Isabella gave birth to ten children. After Isabella's untimely death, Rev. Dobbin remarried a widow, Mary Agnew, who already had nine children of her own! During the mid-nineteenth century, part of the house was used to hide slaves as part of the "Underground Railroad." When the Battle of Gettysburg commenced, the house was used as a hospital.

A psychic entering the Dobbin House told Beth Brett of the appearance of three spirits in the home, one named John, one Mary, and a young Black girl. Apparently, according to some sources, the three are quite friendly and occasionally make their presence known.]

The fireplace that kept the spirits warm that night.

Part of my winter closing routine, as a manager at the Dobbin House Tavern, is to make sure the natural gas fireplaces on the first and second floors of the old house are turned off. There are three fireplaces on the first floor and two on the second floor. During the winter months when these fireplaces are in use, the last thing I do before exiting the house, is to double-check all five fireplaces to make sure they are turned off.

One night during the winter of 1995, two waitresses and myself stayed to close, making our routine sweep of the house before leaving. Even though the lights were off and no glow was detected from any of the fireplaces, all three of us checked each fireplace to make sure they were out. It was the last thing we did and I was the last to exit the building before the alarm was set.

It just so happened that my schedule required me to open the house early the next morning, so our clean-up and prep people could begin working. The alarm was still set and the house was just as I left it. Part of my opening routine that morning took me to the second floor of the house. There, in an otherwise undisturbed area, a roaring fire greeted me! The fireplace on the north end of the house had been turned up full blast! It is with absolute certainty that this fireplace could not have been left on. The night before, three of us checked in on a darkened room and NO flames were evident — let alone the roaring blaze that greeted me the following morning. No person could have been in there without the alarm going off!

Did the spirits turn on the fireplace? If so, why? One can only speculate as to the reason; however, what is certain is that on that particular night the spirits were using a power we cannot explain.

-22-

LOST AND FOUND

[Submitted by: Mark Riley]

I have an unusual story I would like to relate to you — at least unusual in my experience. I belong to a relatively small reenactment group of Confederates from Virginia. While in Gettysburg in June, two friends and I decided to drive to the battlefield in the evening, darkness soon approaching. Aimlessly driving the battlefield, we soon found ourselves in the area of Culp's Hill. Driving slowly, taking in the sights, we had just passed Spangler's Spring when, to our right, someone caught our eye. There, squatting down in front of the Maryland marker, we saw a Confederate soldier — a reenactor, we thought. The soldier was young,

58 caliber bullet found by Mark Riley

very unkempt, and had a good "impression," one every reenactor tries to achieve — the real thing. As we slowly rounded the curve, we continued looking at him and he looked at us. Although it was getting dark, we could see him quite well — his eyes seemed to burn right through us — they were unnerving. We thought it strange to see a reenactor squatting down the way he was, with no one else in sight. Suddenly and abruptly, he stood up and pointed to our left and behind us. We were momentarily taken aback, and quickly turned to see what possible danger he was pointing out. Was it people? Was it a deer? — no, it couldn't be. What then? We all looked intently, but none of us saw nor heard anything. The three of us turned back to the soldier, but to our surprise, he was gone! We thought it was a reenactor playing some sort of trick on us; however, as we rounded the curve, we looked and saw nothing — he was indeed

Maryland Marker.

gone! As we continued our drive over Culp's Hill, the elusive soldier was the topic of our conversation. We finally arrived back in town and decided to stop at a pub for something to drink to settle our nerves. As we continued talking about the experience, one of my friends mentioned that when the soldier quickly stood up, he noticed that something in his hand dropped to the ground. We suggested returning to the spot where we saw the figure to see what the object was; however, it was too dark and besides, tomorrow morning would be soon enough for me. We all agreed. The next morning we drove over to Culp's Hill and found the spot where we saw the soldier the night before. There, in that very spot, was an original 58-caliber mini-ball laying exactly where the ghostly figure dropped it the previous night — or 133 years ago!

–23–

POLTERGEIST PLEAS

[Submitted by: Candice Nemec]

I am relating an incident that happened to me, and ultimately involved my husband, while on the Gettysburg battlefield. My husband, John, and I make a yearly trip to Gettysburg, as we are both Civil War enthusiasts, concentrating on the Battle of Gettysburg. September of 1991 was no exception, as we try to visit the area around September or October to avoid the crowds, and to be able to concentrate on the battlefield without a lot of interference. On this September day, my husband and I had just finished walking around the Soldier's Cemetery. We crossed Baltimore Street and proceeded up the hill to the right of the tour center. As I was walking around, all of a sudden, I stopped and felt as though the temperature had just dropped ten degrees. I had been looking down at the ground and when I looked up I saw a young man — blond, blue-eyed, in his 20's and in a Union uniform. I didn't think a whole lot about it, as I assumed he was a reenactor. He looked at me, pointed down over the hill (in the opposite direction of the entrance to the cemetery) and said, "I'm dead! Help me!" I then glanced over the hill and I could see Confederate soldiers firing upon him. I thought this was great that we were in the middle of a reenactment, and I wanted my husband, who was about 15 feet away from me, to also see this. As I turned to call my husband, I realized the young soldier was gone. I then looked again, down over the hill, and all the Confederate soldiers were also gone. Well, at that point my husband came over to me and said, "What's the matter with you, you are as white as a sheet — did you see a ghost or something?" I realized he was just joking, but I was in no mood to be kidded — I just wanted to get out of there fast! I ran down to the sidewalk and when my husband joined me he asked what was wrong. I proceeded to tell him and I asked him if he saw or heard anything. I felt sure that he must have, because these weren't ghostly, scary, transparent figures, these were solid flesh and blood — or so I thought! My husband immediately wanted me to go back up to the spot and see if the same thing would happen again, to which I said a very forceful "NO WAY — NEVER AGAIN!" We then left and proceeded to go back to our motor home.

After a few days of some serious coaxing by my husband, I finally agreed to go back. As we walked around, it seemed as though everything was normal, then it happened again — the temperature dropped drastically. I asked my husband if he could feel the drop and he said yes, he could. I stood there very still and very quiet for a few minutes to see what would happen next, if anything. When all of a sudden, the young soldier again appeared to me, looking just as real as you or I. This time, as I was still facing him, thinking if I turned away for even a second he might run off. I quietly said to my husband beside me, "There — see! Surely you can see him this time!" To my shock and surprise, my husband saw nothing. Just as before, the young soldier looked at me again and said, "I'm dead! Help me!" At that point, I guess I lost my temper because I very forcefully said, "I will help you if you just tell me what you want!" All during this "conversation" I wasn't completely sure if he was speaking to me or to someone else, in his own "time," and I just happened to be in the way. Just then, he looked at me and I had a tremendous feeling of sadness, as he spoke just one word — "Richter." I said, "I'm sorry, I don't understand. If that is your name, please spell it so I'll know." To my complete surprise — he DID! I then asked him what he wanted me to do with this information, when all of a sudden, he just vanished.

My husband and I left and went to a diner, where I could relate to him what had just happened, and to get a much-needed cup of coffee, as I was quite visibly shaken by what had just transpired. The name the soldier had given me meant nothing neither to myself, nor to my husband. John, who is somewhat an authority on uniforms, ranks, and patches, having been in the Army Reserve for 20 years and a police officer in Pittsburgh for 28 years, tends to focus on those details first. He proceeded to ask me what rank the soldier was, or what patches, if any, he was wearing. I, of course, could not answer because I was much more mesmerized by his face, rather than his uniform. All I could say for certain was that it definitely was a Union uniform.

For a week I tried to find out if there was any way to research the name "Richter". Without knowing what state or rank, it would be very difficult, if not impossible. John and I decided to forget about the

68

incident, finish our vacation, and head back to Pittsburgh.

The rest of September and October I couldn't get the young man out of my thoughts and I kept feeling as though I had to do something — but what? Finally, in November, I pleaded with my husband to take me back to Gettysburg so I could find out more about the young soldier, since the thoughts of him consumed me constantly for almost two months.

Area marked by the **X** is where Candice first encountered Richter.

After much pleading and coaxing, John finally agreed and we returned to Gettysburg. After almost a week of going around in circles and not coming up with anything, we decided to go home the next day. Late in the afternoon of our last day there, I got a strong urge for some unknown reason to go to the Pennsylvania Monument. John reluctantly drove me there, and, after nearly two hours of searching for the name Richter, we were about to leave. Then, very much to my surprise, there it was — the name of one, Tolbert Richter of the 155th Infantry! Could this be the elusive young man I was searching for? I was overjoyed!

Not sure what to do with this new-found information, I asked my husband to take me back to the spot where I initially saw the young soldier. We drove back there and, after what seemed a long time to find the exact site, I finally came upon a significantly colder spot. I stood there for about five minutes and there it was — the angelic face of that young man. I didn't say anything, instead, he looked at me, smiled, and said, "Thank you," nodded his head and vanished. To this day I have not seen him again.

[Author's Note: Since the incident, Candice has been trying to find the meaning behind the sighting of the young soldier and consequently, spent hours researching for a possible answer. Finding out what she could about Tolbert Richter, we know he survived the war and was discharged August 16, 1865, and therefore, was not a casualty of the Battle of Gettysburg.

Intrigued by her story, we decided to search the National Cemetery for the name Richter. Heading toward the Pennsylvania section and after looking at about five graves, we found a Henry Richter. After noting his name, the search continued without any other Richter's being found. Regarding Henry Richter's career, he was inducted into service August 24, 1863, and mustered out July 15, 1865. By the dates, it is obvious he could not have fought in the Battle of Gettysburg. However, one more question arises, since he was not killed in the battle — why is he buried in the Pennsylvania section instead of the veteran's section?

It is known that mistakes were made in the burials in the National Cemetery. For example, to identify a body, belongings in the pockets were checked. Perhaps an object in the pocket belonged to someone else — was borrowed, or picked up — this could lead to misidentification.

What was the young soldier trying to tell Candice with the name Richter? Does he lie in an Unknown grave in the National Cemetery? Is he desperately trying to tell us he does not want to lie forgotten? Is he in a grave with the wrong name? Perhaps we will never know, but then again, will he continue to appear in that cold spot to fulfill his quest?

APPENDIX

The maps on the next two pages show the approximate locations where the stories in this book took place. If, for instance, you are interested in the location of story number 10, *Pickett's Eternal Charge*, look for number 10 on the map. You will see it is near West Confederate Avenue. The second map shows the locations of stories near Devil's Den.

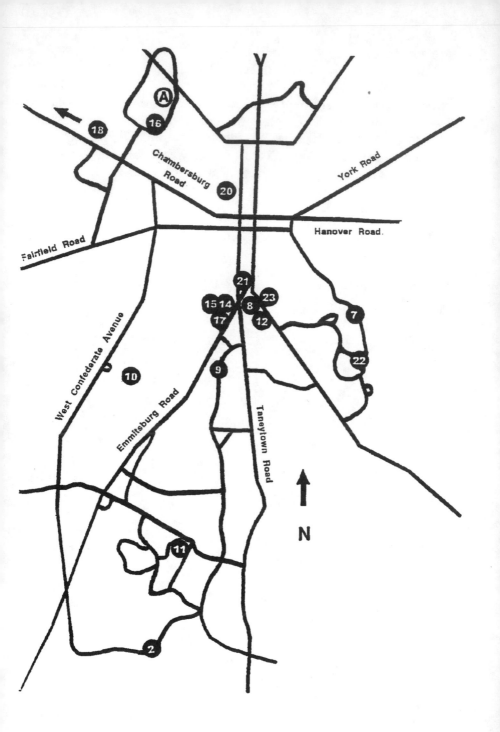

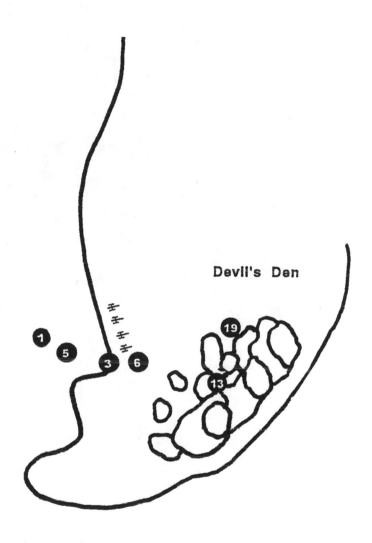

Devil's Den

Have you experienced strange, supernatural, or unexplainable occurrences in Gettysburg? If so, we would like to hear about it for possible inclusion in future publications about Haunted Gettysburg. Please include only first-hand experiences and, if available, photographs you have taken personally. This is your chance to tell your story without fear of ridicule. You are not alone — hundreds, perhaps thousands of people had some sort of unexplained 'ghostly' experience in Gettysburg. If you would like your story told, please fill out and sign the release form and send it to the address indicated for potential inclusion. If your story is used, you will receive a free, personally autographed copy of the book. Your name will be used unless you specifically requested otherwise.

- -

Material/Photo Release

TO: Gettysburg R&D
P.O. Box 4561
Gettysburg, PA
17325

I hereby grant to Jack Bochar and Bob Wasel the absolute right and permission to reproduce the material and/or photographs I have supplied to them for inclusion in Haunted Gettysburg and in future reprints and revisions. I further consent to the publication and copyrighting of this book to be published in any manner they may see fit. Proper acknowledgment of my material and/or photos will be made at the author's discretion.

Name _____

Address _____

_____

_____

Date _____

Signature _____

Shot Glass
$5.00ea.

Embroidered Hat
$15.00ea.

HAUNTED GETTYSBURG

Bumper Sticker
$1.00 ea.

Coffee Mug
$7.50ea.

Sweatshirt
$20.00ea.

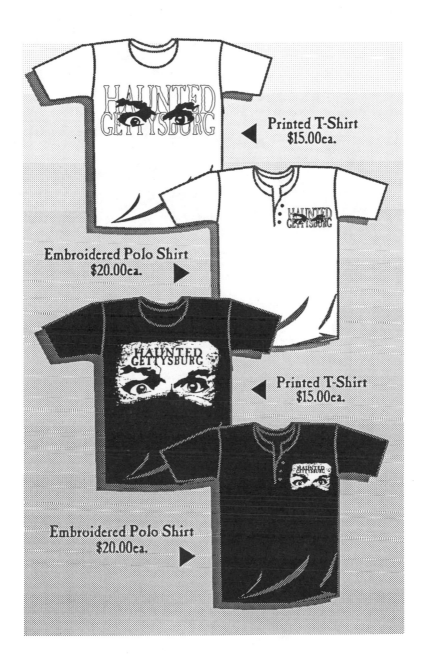

Printed T-Shirt
$15.00ea.

Embroidered Polo Shirt
$20.00ea. ▶

Printed T-Shirt
$15.00ea.

Embroidered Polo Shirt
$20.00ea. ▶

Quantity	Size	Description	Color	Unit Price	TOTAL
		TOTAL			
		$3 SHIPPING & HANDLING 1st ITEM and .50 ¢ EACH ADDITIONAL ITEM			
		GRAND TOTAL			

Thank You for your Order!

HAUNTED GETTYSBURG *ORDER FORM*

call **TOLL FREE:**
1-800-285-5690
Local:
287-5690

MAILING ADDRESS:
Donny Bayne
P.O. Box 3983
Gettysburg, PA 17325

BILL TO:

NAME _____

STREET ADDRESS _____

P.O. BOX _____

CITY _____ STATE _____ ZIP_____

PHONE (__) _____

PRE-PAYMENT METHOD

☐ CHECK ENCLOSED *(Make check payable to Donny Bayne)*

☐ VISA ☐ MASTER CARD

CARD# _____
EXP. DATE: _____
NAME ON CARD: _____